3 4028 08611 8982
HARRIS COUNTY PUBLIC LIBRARY

J B Kane
McClellan, Ray
Kane

$22.95
ocn881386954
02/04/2015

DISCARD

D1606811

WRESTLING SUPERST★RS

KANE

BY RAY McCLELLAN

EPIC

BELLWETHER MEDIA • MINNEAPOLIS, MN

EPIC BOOKS are no ordinary books. They burst with intense action, high-speed heroics, and shadows of the unknown. Are you ready for an Epic adventure?

This edition first published in 2015 by Bellwether Media, Inc.

No part of this publication may be reproduced in whole or in part without written permission of the publisher. For information regarding permission, write to Bellwether Media, Inc., Attention: Permissions Department, 5357 Penn Avenue South, Minneapolis, MN 55419.

Library of Congress Cataloging-in-Publication Data

McClellan, Ray.
  Kane / by Ray McClellan.
    pages cm. – (Epic: Wrestling Superstars)
  Includes bibliographical references and index.
  Summary: "Engaging images accompany information about Kane. The combination of high-interest subject matter and light text is intended for students in grades 2 through 7"– Provided by publisher.
  ISBN 978-1-62617-142-8 (hardcover : alk. paper)
  1. Kane, 1967–Juvenile literature. 2. Wrestlers–United States–Biography–Juvenile literature. I. Title.
  GV1196.J335M33 2014
  796.812092–dc23
  [B]
                            2014011253

Text copyright © 2015 by Bellwether Media, Inc. EPIC BOOKS and associated logos are trademarks and/or registered trademarks of Bellwether Media, Inc. SCHOLASTIC, CHILDREN'S PRESS, and associated logos are trademarks and/or registered trademarks of Scholastic Inc.

Printed in the United States of America, North Mankato, MN.

TABLE OF CONTENTS

WARNING!

The wrestling moves used in this book are performed by professionals.
Do not attempt to reenact any of the moves performed in this book.

THE DEBUT

Kane interrupts a match inside a steel cage. The masked giant rips the door off the cage. Then he enters the ring and stands in front of Undertaker.

UNDERTAKER

Flames shoot from the cage. Kane kicks Undertaker. Then he hits him with a Tombstone Piledriver and leaves the ring. He has made his **debut**.

WHO IS KANE?

NAME-CALLING

★

Kane is nicknamed
The Big Red Monster
because of his size.

Kane is a monster who **terrorizes** other
WWE stars. As a **heel**, he has a mean
streak. This giant wrestler uses his size
and strength to beat opponents.

LIFE BEFORE WWE

BACHELOR OF ARTS

Kane also earned a degree in English Literature.

Kane grew up as a **military brat**. He kept busy playing basketball and football. Later he went to college on a **sports scholarship**.

Kane worked in a **group home** after college.
A coworker there talked him into wrestling.
Soon, Kane became **Doomsday** the wrestler.
He moved to Florida to train.

FIRST JOB

★

Before wrestling,
Kane also worked as
a teacher.

A WWE SUPERSTAR

STAR PROFILE

WRESTLING NAME: Kane

REAL NAME: Glenn Thomas Jacobs

BIRTHDATE: April 26, 1967

HOMETOWN: Madrid, Spain

HEIGHT: 7 feet (2.1 meters)

WEIGHT: 323 pounds (147 kilograms)

WWE DEBUT: 1997 (as Kane)

FINISHING MOVE: Chokeslam

WWE signed him in 1995. He first wrestled under a different name. In 1997, he put on a red mask. He became a half-man, half-monster named Kane.

Kane is often in a **feud**. However, he has partnered with other wrestlers to win more than ten **tag team** championships. He also became a **Triple Crown Champion** in 2001.

UNMASKED

★

In 2003, a loss forced
Kane to remove his mask.
He showed his face
for the first time.

WINNING MOVES

The Chokeslam is Kane's **finishing move**. He locks his hand around an opponent's neck. Then he lifts and throws the opponent to the mat.

POWERSLAM

Kane uses powerslams as **signature moves**. He lifts another wrestler. Then he falls on top of the opponent. Kane crushes him with his weight. Body slammed!

GLOSSARY

debut—first official appearance

doomsday—slang for the day the world ends

feud—a long-standing, heated rivalry between two people or teams

finishing move—a wrestling move that finishes off an opponent

group home—a home where people who need special care live together

heel—a wrestler viewed as a villain

military brat—a child who has one or both parents in the military

signature moves—moves that a wrestler is famous for performing

sports scholarship—an award that gives a student athlete money to pay for college

tag team—a pair of wrestlers who compete as a team

terrorizes—fills with fear

Triple Crown Champion—a WWE wrestler who has won three different championships

TO LEARN MORE

At the Library

Black, Jake. *WWE General Manager's Handbook*. New York, N.Y.: Grosset & Dunlap, 2012.

McClellan, Ray. *Undertaker*. Minneapolis, Minn.: Bellwether Media, 2015.

West, Tracey. *Race to the Rumble*. New York, N.Y.: Grosset & Dunlap, 2011.

On the Web

Learning more about Kane is as easy as 1, 2, 3.

1. Go to www.factsurfer.com.

2. Enter "Kane" into the search box.

3. Click the "Surf" button and you will see a list of related web sites.

With factsurfer.com, finding more information is just a click away.

The images in this book are reproduced through the courtesy of: Albert L. Ortega/ Getty Images, front cover, p. 17; Devin Chen, front cover (small); David Seto, pp. 4, 11, 12; Matt Roberts/ Zuma Press, pp. 5, 16; George Pimentel/ Getty Images, p. 6; Ikuo Hirama, p. 7 (left); Globe Photos/ Zuma Press, pp. 7 (right), 21 (left); WWF/ UPN-TV/ Zuma Press/ Newscom, p. 8; Revelli-Beaumont/ SIPA/ Newscom, p. 9; Wenn Photos/ Newscom, pp. 10, 14; Ed Webster/ Flickr, p. 13; Graeme Taylor/ Zuma Press/ Newscom, pp. 18, 20; Chris Ryan/ Corbis Images, p. 19; Jam Media/ CON/ Getty Images, p. 21 (right).